MY HERO DOESN'T WEAR A CAPE

A tribute to all families who serve in and support the armed forces

Gloria Canada, Ed. D.

Illustrated by Carlos Infante Pompa

innovo
PUBLISHING

Published by
Innovo Publishing LLC
www.innovopublishing.com
1-888-546-2111

![Innovo Publishing logo]

Providing Full-Service Publishing Services for
Christian Authors, Artists, and Organizations: Hardbacks, Paperbacks,

eBooks, Audiobooks, Music, and Film

MY HERO DOESN'T WEAR A CAPE

Library of Congress Control Number: 2014905852
ISBN 13: 978-1-61314-159-5

Cover Design & Interior Layout by Innovo Publishing LLC

Printed in the United States of America

U.S. Printing History
First Edition: April 2014

Dedicated to my father, Charles Herman Canada,
who served proudly and retired from the U.S. Army,
and to my mother, Rosa Canada,
who supported our family throughout our countless moves.

My hero doesn't wear a cape

or stop trains with his bare hand.

His uniform is camouflage,

shades of green and tan.

You see, my dad is in the army, a soldier proud and strong.

He stands up for what is right and fights against what is wrong.

Sometimes when we are walking, strangers come and shake his hand.

They thank him for his service, for protecting our great land.

He can run for miles in deep snow or desert heat.

At home when he does sit-ups, we sit on both his feet.

We often live in quarters, close to families just like ours.

Their moms and dads are soldiers, too, wearing stripes and bars.

We move from post to post and base to base.

That's how our family works.

We get to visit places others only read about in books.

At times Dad goes without us

to far and different lands.

But our mom has lots of courage

and says she understands.

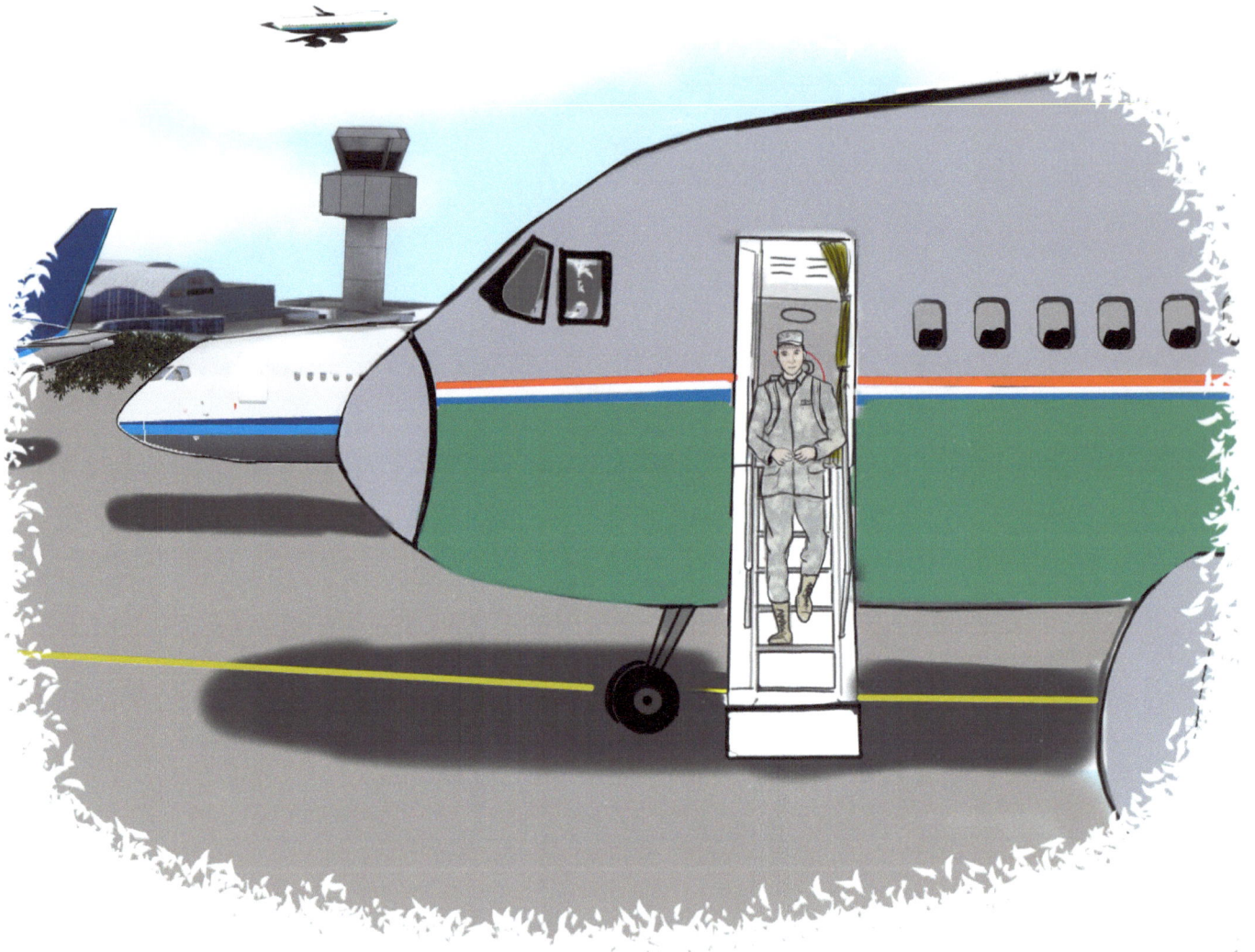

We wait for him to come back home,

to be safe and sound with us.

And when he does,

we celebrate and make a real big fuss!

We watch from the parade stands

as the troops march proudly by.

Our dad is the tall one with the flag held up real high.

We all know the kinds of things an army hero does.

But when our dad's at home,

we have a hero

just for us.

Our hero likes to laugh at the corny jokes we tell.

He even likes the way that little puppies smell.

He always winks at mom and makes her laugh out loud.

He's happy to check our homework and says we make him proud.

His hands are strong and gentle when he tucks us into bed.

He smiles and says, "I love you" and kisses us on the head.

He says he loves this country and
the freedom that it brings.

"God Bless America"
is his favorite song to sing.

He is ready to protect us all so we may live in peace.

He bows his head and prays that all wars will one day cease.

So when you see a soldier on land, in air, or sea,

Know that soldier's a real-life hero,

who's here for you and me.

AUTHOR'S NOTE

My mom clung to the chain link fence; silent tears streaming down her face, as she watched my father walk up the stairs to the airplane. He was on his way to Vietnam. I was twelve years old and the memory still brings a knot to my stomach. My dad was an army soldier. It is no exaggeration to say if you have a mom or dad who serves in the military, the whole family serves.

Only two years earlier, when I was in fifth grade, I remember being in awe of my dad as my mother (wearing a "Jackie Kennedy" pill box hat and white gloves) pinned my dad's new rank on his uniform. He had worked hard, finished his degree and earned the rank of Warrant Officer.

My dad's world changed when he enlisted in the army at the age of seventeen. He began to see the world and loved the army life. Losing his mom as a child, my dad was raised by his aunt, Alcie Hunt, in the comfort and security of the tiny town of Tiptonville, Tennessee. At twenty three, my father spotted my mother working in a bank where he had gone to make a deposit. My mom was a young girl of nineteen who had never made it much further than the city limits where she was raised; the border town of Laredo, Texas. He soon found himself writing a letter to her father requesting her hand in marriage. Against all odds, my parents (from two very different backgrounds) married and raised four children as they traveled from post to post.

Both my parents have passed, but at times I can still hear my dad whistling as he passes the rough brush back and forth across his boots in a certain steady rhythm. One of my earliest memories is watching my dad as he sat cross legged on the living room floor, old newspapers spread out in front of him, where he placed his "spit shined" combat boots to dry after hand polishing them. My mom would be ironing his uniform, spraying on heavy starch to make sure the creases were stiff and straight. They were a true team .

To thank our military for the sacrifices they make for all Americans, the royalties I receive from this book will be donated to organizations which support our military soldiers and their families.

MEET KING GOLDEN AND HENRY THE TULIP BULB

GOD DID MAKE LITTLE GREEN APPLES by Cecelia Assunto is a delightful story with charming characters who teach a simple message about how unkind words and bullying can hurt others deeply. Readers will learn that judging others by their outward appearance is wrong; rather, we should look inward to the heart and always ask ourselves, "What would 'King Golden' do?"

ISBN 978-1-61314-028-4, Paperback, $12.95
Also available in eBook editions.

HENRY'S LIFE AS A TULIP BULB by Linda M. Brandt. Henry the Tulip Bulb was quite content with his comfortable, happy life on a grocery store shelf, so how would he handle all the changes about to take place when two little girls bought him and took him home to plant him in the cold, cold ground? In his unique and charming way, Henry very cleverly shows how to go beyond merely overcoming adversity to actually developing an attitude of gratitude for those hard times in life that tend to challenge us, break us, and ultimately grow us.

ISBN 978-1-61314-082-6, Hardback, $19.95
ISBN 978-1-61314-028-4, Paperback, $12.95
Also available in eBook editions.

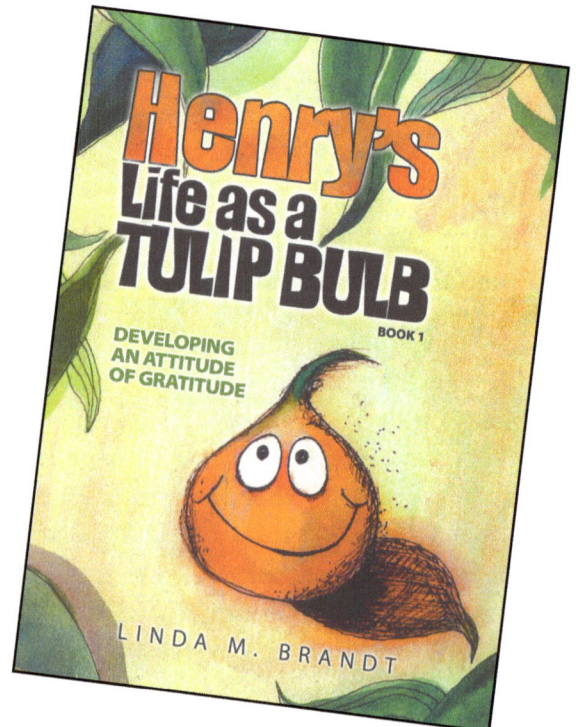

THE LITTLE TOMMY SERIES BY TOM TOOMBS

Little Tommy is five years old. He is energetic, artistic, adventurous, helpful, curious, and compassionate. His dad is a pastor and his mom stays home with him and his two younger siblings. Together with his favorite friend, Bubba, his little hand puppet, he learns valuable lessons in responsibility, friendship, thankfulness, sharing, giving, prayer, and much more. Engaging stories, delightful illustrations, enduring messages. Your child will want to hear them again and again.

THE MYSTERIOUS MONEY TREE: Little Tommy Learns a Lesson in Giving, ISBN 978-1-61314-033-8 Paperback, $12.95, Also available in eBook and Audiobook editions.

THE WAY TO BE A WINNER: Little Tommy Learns a Lesson in Working Together ISBN 978-1-61314-034-5 Paperback, $12.95, Also available in eBook editions.

THE BIG CAMPING ADVENTURE: Little Tommy Learns Lesons from the Great Outdoors ISBN 978-1-61314-035-2, $12.95, Also available in eBook editions.

DAVID, SON OF JESSE by Emily Binning. To most folks he was a kid who would grow up doing just what his family had done for generations before him. But not this David! He grew to become an amazing man with the ability to destroy giants and put enemies of God on the run. And it all began with the love and guidance given by Jesse, David's dad. Jesse loved God and implanted that love into the heart of his youngest son. This story of David weaves a tale that is filled with the adventures of a young man and his father.

ISBN 978-1-936076-20-8, Paperback, $8.95 Also available in eBook editions.

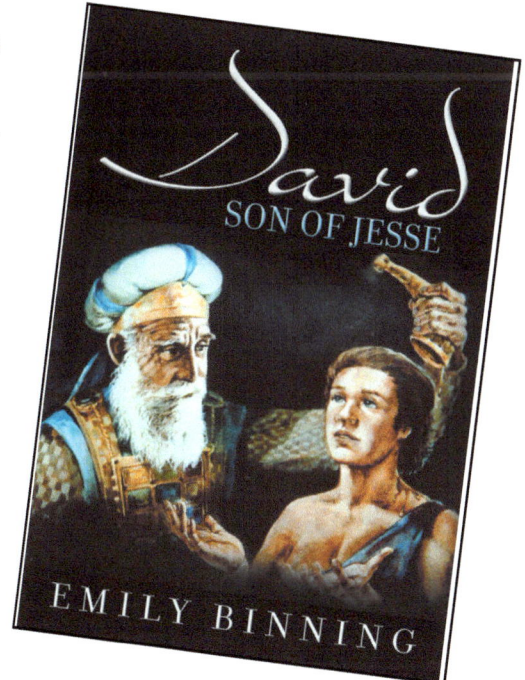

www.ingramcontent.com/pod-product-compliance
Lightning Source LLC
Chambersburg PA
CBHW042007080426
42733CB00003B/38